Lord, I'm Not Smart Enough
Prayers of a Young Mother

Lord,
I'm Not Smart Enough

by
Caroline Gilroy

Beacon Hill Press of Kansas City
Kansas City, Missouri

Dedication

These expressions of faith, love, and confusion
are affectionately dedicated
to the mothers in my life:
Linnie Kirby and Lilla Gilroy,
in gratitude for the patience, guidance, and acceptance
they have offered to me.

Contents

1/I'm Not Smart Enough, Lord

TWO SAINTS prayed for me: "Caroline, you're too smart," one sighed. And the other whispered, ". . . just not smart enough."

Months elapsed between that first prayer and the second one. The first one was spoken before the Holy Spirit cleansed and sanctified my heart; the second after. Funny thing how one can grow from being too smart into the realization of her stupidity in a matter of weeks!

But now, Lord, I do realize that I'm not smart enough for this job of rearing children and caring for my husband as I ought. My heart is purely Yours, perfected by Your grace; but my mind, Lord—my judgment . . .

I need so much more of Your wisdom. I just can't do this thing alone.

What? I don't have to? Thank You, Lord Jesus! I feel better already.

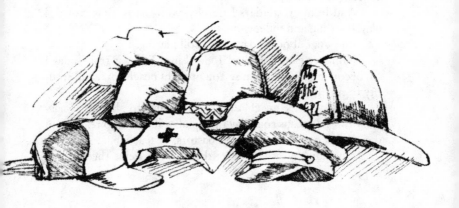

2/These Kids Are Fickle

LORD, these kids You gave me are fickle.

Yesterday morning they went to Sunday School; yesterday afternoon they played church. Today they had their regular checkup with the dentist; tonight they are playing dentist. Tomorrow when they get home from the classroom, I wouldn't be surprised if they decide to play school.

They just can't make up their minds, these kids of mine. They are swept about by the mood of the day.

Oh my! I couldn't be fickle, could I? Not me!

And yet, in my yesterdays, I went with my weekly crowd to the worldly places of entertainment—I played at being sophisticated.

Also in my yesterdays, I attended Sunday School and church—or was I just playing?

And in my yesterdays I traveled with the restless crowd. I played strong and independent.

But what about today? Am I still playing?

No more games, Father! Today I live! Today is real! Today I am becoming me, all because You brought peace, love, and security to my heart.

Father, I hope my children will continue to play their imaginary roles. Perhaps someday their play will turn into reality and they will serve You as dentists, pastors, or teachers . . .

But, Lord, please don't let them play at being themselves.

3/Thank You for the Tender Times

THANK YOU, Lord, for interrupting my reading this evening. The groans, whines, and whimpers that called me to Tabitha's bedside called me to a very blessed moment.

As I tiptoed into her dark room and knelt by her bed, I simply wanted to respond to her cry with love from the heart You have cleansed and claimed. I gently kissed her cheek and asked, "What's wrong, Honey?" I expected to hear tales of a frightening nightmare, a dry mouth, or painful discomfort.

But I could almost see her sweet, satisfied smile even in that darkness, as she replied, "I just wanted to kiss you like you wanted to kiss me."

Father, as I tucked her blankets up around her body, kissed

13

her cheek again, and returned to my special corner, thankful my firstborn had no doubt I would come to her in love, I was reminded that You were waiting for me in our meeting place.

Sometimes, Lord, it seems I am being yanked to pieces as my husband, the kids, the church, and You bid for my attention; but in tender moments such as this, I realize I am a very fortunate person to have so much love stuffed into my hours.

Thank You, Lord, for the tender times. Thank You for people who need me; thank You for love.

4/The Chatter of My Child

TOGETHER WE WALK hand in hand. Our almost-daily trek has become a special time for us, a time we will miss when the classroom claims my child next September.

Generally Charity chatters away as I daydream on these little jaunts down our city streets. She seems satisfied enough with my muttered, all-too-casual responses to her constant roar.

But on the rare occasion, Lord, I hear—I mean I really hear what my little companion is saying; and I stand in awe as she shares with me glimpses of the world she sees from 3'6½" off the ground.

Her spoken thoughts echo, "Mommy, did you hear that

sparrow singing?" Her hushed voice cautions me to travel gently, and I realize I've not heard the natural music for far too long.

"Look at that beautiful butterfly," and wonder illuminates her face as the delicate creature flutters away. Seldom do I take time to "look."

"Those flowers are nice. Can we smell them?" . . . and reverently she reaches out her chubby hand to touch a divinely sculptured blossom. Too long I've tromped by Your flowers, not smelling, not appreciating.

"That robin sure is having a hard time getting his worm out of the ground," and I am aware that I have never seen a robin wrestle with his worm before this delightful moment.

"God sure gave us a nice world to live in, didn't He, Mommy? We should take care of it."

How intelligently my wee one talks as we hike along our city street! Her chatter is that of childlike worship, not childish fantasy. Her heart beats merrily in faith as she sizes up life as it was meant to be, and she adores her Creator through all of her senses.

I guess, Lord, there are times I am not the teacher in our mother-daughter relationship. Sometimes her simple, sincere trust offers wisdom to my soul that far exceeds any I have to offer her.

Thank You, dear Jesus, for this beautiful world You have created so perfectly. Thank You for providing for it so readily! Thank You for the chatter of my child.

5/Little Lights Can Shine BIG!

HOW WIDE were the eyes around our breakfast table this morning, Lord. The dreaded dilemmas and delightful dreams of stepping into a new school year were almost visible as our little scholars sat dwarfed in the high-back dining room chairs.

Tabitha has been reluctantly facing this day all week, wondering how she will know all the things she is supposed to know in Grade Two. Layton merrily skips into every new situation without a thought about its potential hazards. Their mother: well, she is learning to carefully wrap them in prayer. I'm trusting You to see them safely through another nine months of classroom learning.

As they lit their individual candles during our family devotions and whispered their prayers that You would help them let their lights shine in the classroom this year, I knew You were listening. Father, You always listen to them, even if I don't. I am sure Your blessed Holy Spirit captured every request that escaped my little ones' mouths. Thank You for being present at our table, Lord.

Little people are faced with big temptations, but even they can stand firm as long as they are grounded in Your love. Help them let their lights shine. Guide them, Lord!

6/2¢ a Can; 5¢ a Bottle

OUR KIDS have gone into the Pop Can and Bottle Business. For every can they cash in, they get 2¢; for a bottle, they get a nickel! And, Father, did You notice how proud they were as they tithed their first earning last week? (Thank You for reminding me to let each of them put his own envelope in the plate.)

This new business venture is involving all of us now, You know. And even though there are times picking up a discarded container pinches my pride a bit, I try to remember that my kids are more important to me than the opinions of the strangers who curiously observe my activity.

Lord, I pray you will bless the children in this new endeavor, because it is teaching them so much. As their little savings account grows and they make plans for all the Christmas gifts they will buy for each other and for us with it, as they tithe their income on Sunday evenings, as they pack a parcel to their mini-missionary friend brimmed with gifts purchased with their hard-earned money, they are becoming good stewards.

Bless them, Father! They will learn more and more about the joy and excitement of giving and they will learn more and more about You.

At two cents a can; five cents a bottle, they'll never be millionaires, but they will be rich! For they are working to make others happy!

7/I've Taken On Too Much

SOMETIMES I feel like I've bitten off more than I can chew, Lord. Maybe I shouldn't have agreed to accept this job. Don't get me wrong—I love it! But there are times, because I am the one who is responsible for teaching my children many lessons, that I feel like a nag; instead of the sweet, Spirit-filled Mom I long to be.

Who else is there to teach Tabitha, Layton, and Charity the art of tidiness? Their teachers at school expect them to learn that at home!

Who will teach them table manners? I am the one who eats every meal with them, with few exceptions.

Who else cares if they clean their teeth well? Their father and I pay the dentist to fill the holes neglect would create.

Oh, God, I just want to be free to love and enjoy them; but there are so many responsibilities that are mine simply by merit of my role.

Please, Father, teach me Your way of teaching. I never feel nagged by You, yet You expect holy living from me right down to the scruple. I'm the only one, Lord, to teach my children many important lessons.

Please teach me Your way of teaching.

8/No Second Chance!

PERHAPS THE REASON I experiment with basic recipes is because that way no one can tell if I prepared them right or not. If they're original, they can't be wrong.

But once again, Lord, I have been reminded that some things in the kitchen, just like in Your law of living, are basic, not open to my creative touch. There's no way I can repair these silly brownies! If I would have baked them in the right-sized pan, they would have been much yummier, I'm sure. Now my family won't be able to enjoy them to the fullest. The ingredients have been wasted. There is no second chance.

And in this walk, this task of mothering my little ones, I see more than ever that some very basic rules must be followed. You permit me to be creative with the way some rules are carried out, true; but You insist that they *must* be carried out!

Sometimes, Father, it would be easier to let my little ones do as they please; but Your Basic Law says a child shouldn't be left to his own understanding. Sometimes I'm too tired to correct disobedience; but Your Basic Law says I must be faithful to apply the rod if I am going to help them be all You intend for them to be.

There's so much I must do right the first time around. I know there's no second chance!

These should-be brownies won't matter a lot in eternity, even though I do regret the waste. But the value of the hours I spend with my charges this day will matter! Help me to add the right ingredients; to mix them with love, and to allow plenty of room for Your Spirit to warm their hearts . . . for Jesus' sake. Amen!

9/The Lessons I Want to Teach My Children

LOOK AT THEM, LORD, they are so young, so impressionable. Before their years have swept them off into eternity, Tabitha, Layton, and Charity have many lessons to learn. I long to teach them these lessons now. I would like to teach them

- to face disappointments honestly, without succumbing to self-pity
- to face fear openly, without losing trust in the guardianship of their Heavenly Father
- to acknowledge they have been hurt, without letting bitterness grow in their hearts

25

- to accept success, without letting pride get out of proportion
- to accept failure, without accepting defeat
- to want, without coveting
- to voice their honest opinions, without being obnoxiously opinionated
- to stand firm in their convictions, with or without support from others
- to be flexible, without being wishy-washy
- to know laughter, but not at the expense of their fellowman
- to appreciate and enjoy the beautiful and delightful things in this world, without letting the accumulation of these things become all-important
- to be alone, without being lonely

Father, I can begin the lessons, but I can teach them only in part. But when *He* that is perfect has come, they will learn in whole. Teach them, Lord Jesus; teach them, I pray!

10/Where Are the Edges

THE VEGETABLE SOUP was hot. The steam rolling off the wee alphabet noodles left no doubt of that. I told the kids that the secret of eating a torrid dish is to scoop out bites from the edges where the soup has had a chance to cool!

But, Charity, Lord—she sometimes has problems understanding these scientific facts. After the lunch was blessed, everyone else began eating. Looking up, Charity simply asked, "Mommy, where are the edges?"

And today, Father, I am having trouble finding the edges too. I just don't seem to know how to begin to gently scoop my children up out of the dismal atmosphere of this chaotic world. Today I'm just not sure I can find the right way of helping them

27

develop into happy, well-adjusted human beings. The steam of a discontented, anything-goes-world will blind their childish eyes if I fail.

I don't understand all I hear You saying at times, but I trust Your love and Your wisdom. Show me where to begin. Father, in childlike faith, I am looking to You. Tell me, Lord, where are the edges?

11 /Did You Laugh, Lord?

I WONDER, did You laugh when Tabitha prayed? Looking back, I can see some humor in it. I can hear her now: "Thank You, God, for the ride. Please help us get back to shore safely."

We did enjoy our last big family summer outing. I am thankful for Your warm sunshine, for the lovely park where we walked, for the roaring fire where we roasted our hot dogs, for the rowboat, the calm stream.

In the middle of all these blessings, why should Tabitha express such concern? Granted, her daddy and I are not the world's greatest boatmen; but there wasn't any big emergency. We were only going around and around in the middle of the river.

29

The other two kids were so sweet as they prayed their, "Thank You, Jesus, for this fun afternoon; for parents who love us; for the boat ride . . ."

Tabitha's "Please help us get back to shore safely," didn't stir my sentiments as I would have liked. Somehow I felt my pigtailed wonder was missing out on the whole purpose of our prayer pause. But now, Father, I can smile about her honesty. She is learning to trust You for everything. Her mommy needs to be a little bit more like her!

For this day, I too give thanks. And by the way, Lord Jesus, please help me get my children to the other shore safely! Amen.

12/How Many Riddles Should I Answer?

ARE YOU GETTING TIRED of the same old riddles, Father? After all these centuries, You should be! I can't believe my son is trying to stump me with the same questions I thought were original when I was nine. But he is!

How his big brown eyes sparkle as he shares his latest joke with me. "Get it, Mom? Get it?" he blurts. Sometimes I am tempted to reply, "I got it 20 years ago!"

But here's the riddle that is puzzling me these days, Lord: How many of Layton's jokes should I answer correctly? After all, I don't want him to discover I am not the genius he believes me to be. On the other hand, I don't want to discourage him with too much brilliance. Perhaps he wouldn't even bother sharing

31

his jokes with me if I did that. Perhaps he would be discouraged from sharing any of his thoughts with me.

How many riddles should I answer? That's a new one for me, Lord, but I suppose it's as old as the ages for You. That's why I feel confident You will guide me, even in this small matter.

Thank You, Father, for not getting tired of the same old riddles!

13/Sometimes I Forget

CHARITY seems happy enough with the results of this morning's baking endeavor. But I am still a bit dissatisfied. A slight trace of my own growing pains is hovering over these afternoon hours.

My little princess enjoys special work times with me, Lord. I enjoy them, too, but sometimes I forget that these minutes spent chattering, cracking (smashing?) eggs, and dumping flour are some of my most valuable minutes of the day. Preoccupied with the thoughts of domestic chores I want to accomplish before evening is here, I forget and rush her.

Father, I'm so ashamed when I show impatience. As clumsy hands pressed the fork down on our experimental peanut butter goodies, I wanted her to do it fast, but right. I forget how little she is. I expect big things of her. Jesus, I do forget that she loves me, and because of that love she usually gives every job her best, her perfect effort.

Even though she doesn't seem to notice that her mommy is performing less than perfectly during these sessions, I notice. It hurts. I really do love having her help me.

Father, as Your child, I long to have You accept my bungling attempts to complete daily assignments. I am secure in Your love, for You always remember I am human. You understand my limitations.

She's only four, Lord. Sometimes I forget. Please help me remember!

14/Special, but Not Superior

FATHER, I am in a quandary. I want to teach my children an eternal truth, but I don't know how to go about it. How do I let them know they are very, very special people without making them feel they are superior?

I want them to know they are different because they are unique individuals—but I don't want them to think they are odd.

I want them to know they are talented, clever, wonderful; but I want them to also know that without You they can do nothing worthwhile.

Father, how do I teach them they are important, while letting them know they are unworthy of the Gift You offer them?

How do I get the message across to them that they are responsible to fill unique places in their world because You have given them so very much.

Lord, to me they are the best! I want them to know it. I want them to know know they are special. But I don't want them to feel superior.

Tell me, humble Jesus, how do I teach them all of this in one short childhood?

15/Fit Them Well

THIS MORNING Charity came forth with Tabitha's Road Runner sneakers on her feet. What a funny sight watching her clomp about the living room, literally tripping over her own feet, or at least over the shoes on those feet. A few trips around the house convinced her that her own sneakers were not only more comfortable but also far easier to maneuver.

I agree with Charity's decision, Father. Filling someone else's shoes is a tricky, next to impossible task. Thank goodness, You are an understanding cobbler.

I realize I wasted much effort in past years trying to be what I thought other people expected me to be. Awkwardly, I fell all over myself trying to be more sophisticated or more spiritual or more youthful or more with it.

But You knew that down in my heart of hearts, I simply wanted to wear the shoes fitted for my soul! You knew I longed to laugh, cry, and love from the depths of me—to soar to the heights of my spirit, to dream lofty dreams, and to reach for the stars!

Thank You for making it possible, Lord! Because of Your grace in my heart, I am free to be me. My soul is neither floundering around in shoes too big, nor is it being pinched by those too small. The me You designed for my spirit fits perfectly, and I shall endeavor to become that me!

Oh, Lord, fit my children with the personalities suited just for them and give them the grace to wear them well.

This I ask in the name of Your Son who was comfortable being Jesus Christ! Amen and Amen!

16/Thank You, for Second-place Prize

THANK YOU, Father, for allowing Charity to win the second-place prize for me in this Mother's Day Coloring Contest. Even though I'm not one much for sweet-smelling perfumes and powders, thank You for the talent that enabled her to compete and to win.

My ponytailed pet is so very proud of her self-earned gift, and I am so proud of her! But I am aware of the task You have given me. I am once again humbled, for I realize, Lord, that You've given my little elf numerous talents—multiplied abilities—and I know they have been granted to her for one

39

major purpose: that she might be a part of the great task of Kingdom building. In this minute, I have been reminded anew that much of her early development rests in my clumsy hands. I know I must be her first-years' sculptress—I must help plant a longing in her heart to develop every skill, reach for excellence, and then to give all she has back to You.

O Father, help me to guide her as You would have me to. Show me how to instill heavenly goals into her impressionable heart, so that one day, she will be a laborer in Your vineyard.

Hear my request, I pray.

Amen!

17/The Black Bottom Crest

AT LEAST THREE WEEKS have faded into history, Lord, and Tabitha is still requesting prayer that she will find that "Black Bottom" crest. You'd think our pigtailed princess would simply accept the fact that it's gone and forget about it. But she was so proud of earning that badge that never even got home, let alone sewn onto her favorite jacket.

We have tried to reason with her, Father. We've told her it is probably long gone; that You have a better plan. But she still believes You will bring it back. Perhaps she believes better than her mommy who would give up hope. To be honest, I don't know what we are to say to her or ask You for in all of this.

Lord, it is just a silly sports crest—nothing too important, except to my Tabitha. I know You know where it is, even at this very moment. I know You care about Tabitha . . . that You love her even more than I do. If You have a faith-lesson for her to learn through this, then do whatever it will take to teach her.

But, if it's just a matter of one "Black Bottom" crest being located; please, please answer my little one's prayers. She believes Your promises. She has prayed a prayer of faith. She trusts Your love. Show her mommy how to pray as well . . .

Father, Your will be done, that's all I ask, even in the matter of one, nonessential Black Bottom crest!

Amen!

18/How Do They Know What Gifts to Buy?

IT'S REALLY AMAZING, Lord. Tell me, how do my children always know what gifts I will enjoy? Do they have a sixth sense? Some supernatural leading?

Just take the "Mom, Mom, Mom" mug Charity chose for me all on her own. Even though I have a vast selection of mugs, how did she know that one would become my favorite when she picked it from the shelf?

And Tabitha's blue candle was just what I wanted, once I saw it. How her eyes sparkled as I told her so!

Layton, the more practical shopper, knew his mommy does a lot of writing. Such a special pen he chose for me!

But, how do they know mommy like mugs, candles, pens? Surely You, the great Gift-Giver planted the ideas in their hearts—and mine. Help me to always be genuinely pleased with their offerings, whether they be painted rocks, a shabby array of flowers, or candles. Help me to remember how important it is to me for You to accept my humble offerings . . .

Thank You, Lord Jesus, for this beautiful day of receiving, this day of seeing my children made so happy through my happiness.

But, tell me, how did my little ones know what gifts would make this such a perfect day for me?

19 / My Beautiful Girls

THEY ARE BEAUTIFUL, my girls. Just listening to their senseless chatter and spontaneous giggles brings such joy to my heart, Lord, that I can't help but praise You for their perfect bodies and bright minds.

Father, I stand amazed at how different our daughters are. Even though they both have our blood racing through their veins, they are so very different.

Tabitha with her flowing ash-blond hair bounces into my presence and bounces out again, radiating perpetual joy. Charity is my chunky, moody, golden ponytailed elf. Cuddles and sugars are her substance.

Father, I love my children equally, but I love them in different ways. Help me to note and admire their uniqueness. Please help me to love them better as individuals . . . not as a part of a set. Lord, if I'm tempted to compare them, please stop me short. Make Your cautioning voice ever heard.

I too long to be free to be me in Your family. Even though I have numberless brothers and sisters in Christ, Your blood flows through us all; You created me with a unique personality, different talents.

Lord, teach me to give my girls the freedom You've given me through Your love. As Your child, I ask . . .

20/Surprised by the Inevitable!

WELL, FATHER, the inevitable has happened. I guess I knew it could, but I still wasn't prepared for it. Perhaps my being caught off guard is why I reacted so harshly to Layton's whimpers about being teased because he is a preacher's kid.

Poor Layton! I listed all the reasons he should be *delighted* to be a pastor's child. I knew as soon as my little lad's sobbing protest began that there was no good excuse for reacting as I did. "But, Mommy, that's not what I mean. I'm not sorry I'm a pastor's son! It's just that it hurts when they tease me."

O Lord, You understand my hurts. Without condemning me, You help me to see through my pain. You never chide me for feeling pain others have inflicted on me. You never allow self-pity, but You allow pain. Please teach me to do the same for my children. Teach me to comfort them when their anguished spirits cry out. Help me to encourage them to see beyond their pain, to find healing in You.

I hope Layton understood my feeble apology. I hope he understood "I'm human too, Layton." I hope he never ceases to share his deepest thoughts with me, even if I goof on occasion. And I truly do hope he knows what a privilege it is to be a part of a parsonage family.

Father, I need Your wisdom, especially when I am surprised by the inevitable.

21/When I Say I'm Sorry . . .

SHE HAS BEEN such a stinker lately that I have found it hard to believe she's serious when she says, "I'm sorry."

But through this picture she laboured so tediously over in the recluse of her room, You have once again come to teach me. For as I view her crude drawing of herself kneeling beside her bed I read her words, "When I say I'm sorry, I really am sorry." You have helped me understand my pigtailed princess a wee bit better.

Thank You for reminding me that once I too was naughty. Once I was less than what Your love intended me to be and could make me to be. How hard it was for me to live a life of joy and peace with a battle raging within me, and how sorry I was every time the conflict surfaced.

You knew I was sorry. You understood my double-mindedness. Lord, thank You for graciously applying Your love to my heart, for accepting me as I offered my confused life to You. Thank You for patiently forgiving me even today when I fail to perform as one who has been cleansed, even though obedience is now the single desire of my being.

Thank You for reminding me of all of this in these minutes so I can understand Tabitha's problem better!

22/Thank You!

I DON'T HAVE ANY IDEA why Charity should think the big boys would chase her today. Do You, Lord?

As we chatted about her upcoming day at kindergarten, Charity expressed that fear.

"Do they usually chase you?" I wanted to know.

Her "No, but they might," was followed shortly by a "Will you pray for us, Mommy?"

I don't know why Charity was frightened, but I do understand, because many times the enemy has sifted joy from the hours of my day by presenting silly notions to my head. So often I have wasted precious hours fretfully looking to the future, instead of praising You for the warm memories of the past and the pleasantness of the present.

Tonight, Father, I need to thank You for answering prayer. I need to thank You that in our nation we are free to love You; I need to thank You that my little ones are not going hungry; that You have provided so very bountifully for our needs. I need to thank You that my husband travels safely in his car, mile after mile. I need to thank You that no big boys tormented my little girl on her way to school today.

When I told Charity, "Mommy prayed for you." Her simple reply was "Thank you."

Tonight, Lord, that's my simple phrase of adoration for keeping us through another day. Thank You! Thank You!

23/Silliest
on the Sabbath

THEY ARE SILLIEST on the Sabbath. I don't know why that's so, but it does seem to be the pattern our little ones have fallen into.

And to be honest, Lord, after feeding Your sheep all day, we are too tired to enjoy our frolicking little lambs as we would like. By the time we make it through Sunday School and worship in Markdale; and then drive to worship in Feversham, we feel a real need to relax and slow down a bit before the evening service. But the children don't seem to have that same desire, Lord. As a matter of fact, they seem to be just getting going good by Sunday afternoon.

Lord, our kids enjoy life every day of the week. And I suppose it is appropriate that they would enjoy it most on Sunday. I don't want to discourage their joy with my weariness.

Father, You know their needs, and You know ours. You know we don't want to grouch and grump at them, especially on the day we have set apart as holy. On days when we are tired, so very tired as the hours unravel, perhaps You could give them a little less energy and us a bit more. Better yet, maybe You could bless us all with more love to enable us to recognize each other's feelings.

Lord, help me to be the happy mommy they need me to be on this busy day of worship; and help them to understand that Daddy and I are tired. Your healing can take place for us all, even on the Sabbath.

24/What a Difference a Day Makes!

TWENTY-FOUR HOURS certainly can make a big difference when one is adjusting to the news that she will wear glasses, is seven years old, and is afraid of being teased. It's amazing, Lord, what a difference one day can make in the life of a little one who has asked You for strength.

I expected You to help Tabitha through this traumatic experience, Father, but I have to admit I am surprised by how well You helped. I never expected to hear her beam, "I'm excited about wearing glasses now." But tonight, after a day in school, she has a whole new attitude.

Lord, my little girl has learned to turn to You so readily for the help she needs to face disappointments. As I cradled her sobbing form in my arms, I too was praying. You could rearrange her thinking. She needs the glasses to see clearly; and, Lord, doing well in her schoolwork depends on seeing well. She needs to study correctly to prepare herself to serve You to the best of her ability, and she needs to serve You, because You died for her.

Thank You, Lord, for changing Tabitha's mind. Thank You for the difference this day has made in her life.

25/They Are Beginning

LORD, I THINK my little ones are beginning to understand intercessory prayer in a deep, childlike way. I think they are beginning to be truly touched by the pain others bear, and I praise You that this is so.

After Layton asked for prayer for his headache this morning, I was not surprised my girls wanted to pray for him right then. *We* taught them to do that. But Charity's simple, "Help Layton's head feel better, because I know it's not fun to have a headache . . ." came from training she has received at Your nail-scarred feet. I praise You for setting Your perfect prayer pattern before her.

Jesus, as my children grow in years, I have one deep-seated desire: that they will also grow in grace. I long for them to truly know how to serve You by serving others. In the hours of this day I have been made humbly aware that they can learn to do that only as You, the suffering servant, live in them. There's such a long way to go! But with Your help, I know they will make it, all the way to Calvary.

Tonight I lift my heart in praise. Layton's headache went away, and You know even better than me, "it's no fun to have a headache." Thank You for answering my children's prayers.

26/You Understood . . .

YOU UNDERSTOOD the pain I felt this morning as I sent Charity crying out the door on the way to school, didn't You, Lord? You knew the agony my heart was enduring as I watched her little legs stumble along, so desperately trying to catch up with her older brother and sister so that she would not have to walk alone. (How deeply it must pain You when You must discipline me!)

You knew that I wanted her to catch up with them, that I didn't want her to suffer. But I am assured that You also knew how many times she had been told to speed up so that she would not cause Tabitha and Layton to be late for their classroom activities. You knew that I had told her I would let them leave without her. Idle threats are damaging to my children. I had to

59

follow through on promises made, instead of wasting time nagging them. How else can they learn to become the responsible individuals You intend for them to be?

Lord, it is not always fun being a mother—it was not fun this morning; but it does help to know You were there . . . You cared . . . You understood.

27/Thank You for My Treasures!

I SURE DO HOARD rare treasures, don't I, Father? Treasures like that first lock of curly hair clipped from Charity's head; worthless cards and pictures created by Tabitha's uncoordinated plump hands that could barely hold a crayon in their grip—this first love-note written by my very, very special son.

I had forgotten about it, but there it was tucked away in my wallet; always near, yet unknowingly so. I can still remember the night Layton scribbled those lines. The missionary meeting had gotten too long and boring for my little six-year-old son so he laboured over this expression of love for me: "Mather. Mather day I love Mam Its form Layton I love Mamy and I love Curady and I love Tubsa and I love watr and I love Aunt Mry and I love Grama haggy Mather bay."

God, I'm so thankful for that note that I rediscovered in these hours. I'm so thankful for the spontaneous burst of affection that has flowed through my being during these moments of remembering.

Layton's spelling and grammar have matured over these four years. His penmanship has changed and so have many of his thoughts. But I pray that his love for me will never change. I want it to grow—deepen, but never change. In his childlike way, he rendered a perfect and free expression of the feelings he held for his family that cool spring evening four years ago. I pray he will always love us in that sweet way.

Father, I do thank You for all the treasures that are mine as a mother . . . Charity's first lock of hair; Tabitha's artistic creations . . . thank You for this love note written by my very special son.

28/For Mothers Everywhere!

LORD JESUS, in these sacred minutes I have simply come to pray. First, I have come to thank You for the privilege of being a mother. As I look into the tiny faces I adore, I wonder, who am I that I should be given such an honored position as I walk this side of heaven? Thank You, Jesus, for my children.

And thank You, Jesus, for the mother You gave me. Thank You for her support, confidence—thank You for the sacrifices she made for me through the years.

I have also come to thank You for sanctifying my heart while Tabitha, Charity, and Layton were so young, for opening my eyes to Your plan before their lives had been smothered by my selfishness. Thank You for pursuing me until I was captured by Your love! Thank You for love that passes all understanding.

And now, Lord, I would also come on behalf of mothers everywhere; those in all walks of life, every frame of mind. I come on behalf of the lonely, the holy, the poor, the sinful. I come asking for Your love to reach them that they may know the joy I've discovered at the foot of Your cross! Help them, Lord, to know Your will for the role they must play in the lives of their children.

For the expectant mothers I also come, Father, asking that as their child grows in their bodies You would plant noble ideals in their hearts. Help them to set their motherly goals high. Give them zest, patience, energy, wisdom, humility. Grant them all they will need to be the mother they long to be as they dream about the day they can cradle their child in their arms.

Mothers who have opened their homes and hearts to children not born to them have special needs, Father. Please touch their lives in a unique way and show them how important is the role You have chosen for them. Help them to understand themselves and their feelings, honestly open themselves to Your insights, and cast off unmerited guilt feelings that would hinder them from being the mother You intend them to be.

Lord Jesus, help us mothers everywhere. Grant us Your knowledge day by day, minute by minute. Teach us to be loyal to our calling, to be true to Your cause in the confines of our homes as well as in the vastness of the world away from home.

Teach us to believe in our children even when there seems to be no reason to believe in them. Teach us to be firm, but tender—teach us what is to be endured and what is not to be endured—teach us the grace of laughter—grant us compassionate tears for wayward little souls.

All of this and more, Lord, teach us. Guide us as we do this job You have assigned to us. Teach us, Lord, teach us, for we humbly admit we are not smart enough to do this job alone!